ALL ABOUT US

BOOKS BY EVA KNOX EVANS

(Published by G. P. Putnam's Sons)

Jerome Anthony
Araminta
Araminta's Goat
Key Corner
Skookums
Emma Belle and Her Kinfolks
The Lost Handkerchiefs

(Published by Grosset & Dunlap)

A Surprise for Araminta

(Published by D. C. Heath)

Something Different

(Published by Hinds, Hayden & Eldredge, Inc.)

Let's Raise Pigs
Let's Cook Lunch
The Doctor is Coming
Dress Up your School
School Can Be Fun
Let's Plant Grass
Let's Get Together
Out Under the Sky

ALL ABOUT US
by EVA KNOX EVANS
Illustrated by VANA EARLE

CAPITOL PUBLISHING COMPANY, INC.

Copyright MCMXLVII by
CAPITOL PUBLISHING COMPANY, Inc.

Twelfth Printing—1957

Published by Capitol Publishing Company, Inc.
139 Fifth Avenue, New York 10, N. Y.
Manufactured in the United States of America

A STATEMENT

The struggle for an unprejudiced attitude towards the simple and yet so often misunderstood facts of human existence must start at the still flexible mind of the child. "ALL ABOUT US" is a courageous and helpful effort in this direction.

PROFESSOR ALBERT EINSTEIN

Institute for Advanced Studies
Princeton, N. J.

People are important

CONTENTS

CHAPTER I
About Starting Off and Going Places

CHAPTER II
About the Way We Look

CHAPTER III
About the Way We Act

CHAPTER IV
About Americans

CHAPTER V
About Our Friends

To Boris, a rather new American, because I am so glad he came.

About
STARTING OFF AND GOING PLACES

CHAPTER 1

The air was filled with noise and dirt

PEOPLE BEGAN A LONG TIME AGO

so long ago that no one at all knows just when. In those times the world was not such a crowded place. But, of course, through the thousands of years that followed there were more and more people. And during these thousands and thousands of years the people did not stay in one place. They traveled.

They traveled, not because they had an itch for going places, but because there was no other way to keep alive.

For in that time so long ago it was not an easy thing to find enough food to eat. The early men knew nothing about planting seeds and harvesting vegetables. They ate the food they found in the places where they were, and when it was gone, they moved on.

It was not an easy thing to find a safe place to live. Wild animals sometimes came on a most unfriendly visit, and the people would have to run for their lives.

Or a mountain might suddenly begin to spout fire and hot molten rock. The rivers that came down from that mountain would boil and churn and sizzle. No one could stay alive in the path of a volcano.

Rains that poured in blinding torrents might have washed them out of their homes. Sun beating down on a land where the rains never seemed to come might have sent them wandering to find a greener, shadier place.

As the people traveled they probably tried to stick together. It was safer that way, and besides it is so dreadful to be lonely. But things were always happening so that some of the crowd would get separated from the others.

There are always differences of opinion, and there may have been some of the people who wanted to stay in one particular grassy place at the very time that some of the others wanted to find a better place.

And there are always people who are not quite as daring as other people, so that deep and surging

This is the way people traveled

rivers might make some decide to stay on one side, while the others crossed over.

Then, too, a group of people might come to a place where there was not quite enough food to go around. So some of the people would throw stones at the other people, and some of them would go skedaddling to find another place to live.

Or, as sometimes happened when the world was

new, the earth would give a great heave. A split would appear in the ground with water churning up out of it. Some of the people would be on one side of the deep gulley, and some of the people would be on the other side, with no way to get across.

And so they walked their separate ways.

That is the way people traveled and got spread over this round world of ours.

These were the people who were our
great-
        great-
                who-can-tell-how-many-greats-
grandmothers and grandfathers!

LET'S SUPPOSE

that some of these people had names just as you and I have. We don't know whether they called each other anything or not, but there is nothing to keep us from doing it.

Mama and Papa Gog and their children, and Mama and Papa Sog and their children, with some cousins and some uncles and some aunts, went out one morning to dig for roots. There on the little hill opposite them they could see Mama and Papa Siggle and their children, and Mama and Papa Biggle and their children, with some nieces and nephews and brothers-in-law, looking for sharp stones.

Nobody can imagine what they said to each other. Maybe they smiled and waved, for all of these families were traveling and living together.

Suddenly there was a low rumble from the top of the mountain high above them. Papa Gog looked up from his hillside. Pape Siggle looked up from his hillside. They looked but they couldn't see anything. They listened and they still could hear that low rumble. It was not a sound they had ever heard before. There were many things happening each day and night that they could not explain. So they all went on working.

Almost at once, with a great crashing and banging, the air was filled with noise and dirt and dust. Great stones hurtled down from the mountain top, bringing trees and boulders and logs and anything else that got in their way.

There was no time for the Gogs and the Sogs to call out to the Siggles and the Biggles. There was no time for anything at all but to get out of the way of that crashing mountain land which had so suddenly begun to move and rush toward them.

And after, when the noise had stopped, when the rocks and trees were still, through the haze of dust and dirt there was no way to see from one hillside to the other hillside. There was no way to get across either. No path could be made, no tunnel dug through.

The Gogs and the Sogs and their children with their cousins and their uncles and their aunts were on one side. The Biggles and the Siggles with their children and their nieces and their nephews and their brothers-in-law were on the other side.

And so they wandered, each crowd in its own direction. The Gogs and Sogs traveled. They married, and they had children, and there were more and more people in their group. They tried to stay together, although they found that they couldn't always do that.

Many of them wandered hundreds of years until they came to the hot and sunny skies of the equator. There some of them stayed for thousands of years. As they lived there through the ages with their children and their children's children, for some reason their looks began to change. Their skin became brown; they lost the hair on their bodies; the hair on their heads became very black and curly.

The Siggles and the Biggles were traveling too. They also married and had children and more children and cousins and uncles and aunts in their families. Quite by accident as they traveled, they went toward the north where the skies are cold and blue. And for some reason, as they lived there through the ages, the hair did not leave their bodies, their skins became whitish, and their head hair—which was not so curly—became blond.

Of course, not all of the people went to the north

with the Siggles or to the south with the Sogs. We don't know how they got there, but some of the early people settled in an entirely different place. They stayed in what we now call Asia and lived there for thousands and thousands of years. Their looks began to change too. They lost the hair on their bodies; their skin became yellowish tan. Their head hair became black and very straight, and a fold of skin grew across one corner of their eyelids, giving their round eyes a sort of almond shape.

None of these families of people looked the way their grandmothers and grandfathers had looked in the very beginning when they had all started on their travels.

For when people stay together such a long time in the same place, they begin to look and act alike. They eat the same kind of food. They live in the same kind of houses under the same kind of sky in the same kind of weather. They do the same things in the same kinds of ways.

When they marry, their children look like their

parents. Their grand-children and great grand-children usually look like them too, until finally all of them may have brown skins and curly black hair like the Gogs and Sogs. Or they might have whitish skins and straight blond hair like the Siggles and Biggles, or yellowish-tan skins and straight hair like the people in Asia.

But when these people get broken up, and separate, and stay separated for hundreds of years, they begin to look and act different.

MUCH, MUCH LATER
when men had learned to build boats, they began to go on trips. They went on trips to buy the things they needed. They went on trips to see what they could see.

The Siggles began to meet the Sogs, and the Biggles began to meet the Gogs, and the Siggle-Sogs got acquainted with the Biggle-Gogs. You would never have guessed how surprised all of them were!

The Sogs had got so used to seeing people with

brown skins and black wooly hair that they didn't like to look at the Siggles with that pale white skin. They thought white skin made people look sick and ugly. They thought that only people who looked like *them* were pretty.

The Siggles meet the Gogs

Of course, when the Siggles got a good look at the Gogs, they thought: "Whoever heard of anyone with brown skin?" It looked dirty. For you see, they thought that only people who looked like *them* were pretty.

The Biggle-Gogs were disgusted with everyone who didn't have their nice slant eyes and their round

faces with no ugly nose stuck way out in front. For they, too, thought that anyone who didn't look like *them* was ugly.

And that's the way it is sometimes with us.

The Sogs and the Siggles meet the Biggle Gogs

The Chinese think Europeans look very funny with such sharp noses and narrow, pointed faces. The Africans think that white people look pale and thin and ought to be put right to bed until they get over being sick. Some Europeans think that only blond hair and blue eyes are pretty; other Europeans think that mellow black eyes and glossy black hair are the only kind to have.

For all of us get used to seeing people who look a certain way, and we think that is the only way to look.

But no matter what kind of nose we have, or what kind of skin, or whether our hair is curly or straight we all had the very same great-

                              great-

                                          it's-anybody's-guess - how - many - greats - grandmothers and grand-fathers!

About
THE WAY WE LOOK

CHAPTER II

Wouldn't it be silly if we all looked alike

All About Us

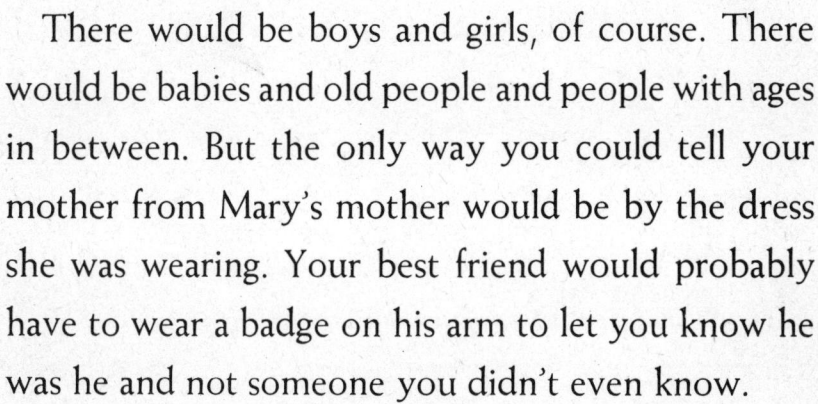

WOULDN'T IT BE SILLY

if we all looked alike?

There would be boys and girls, of course. There would be babies and old people and people with ages in between. But the only way you could tell your mother from Mary's mother would be by the dress she was wearing. Your best friend would probably have to wear a badge on his arm to let you know he was he and not someone you didn't even know.

Mothers wouldn't dare leave their babies outside of grocery stores in their baby carriages, because how could they be sure they had the right one when they came out?

Ladies would not have to buy powder and lipstick and nail polish to make themselves look like movie stars, because they *would* look like movie stars!

Of course, teachers would not be able to tell any of the children in their classes apart, and you might get blamed for something you hadn't done at all.

Meeting your aunt at the railroad station would be no fun at all. For she would look like every other forty-year-old aunt in the whole world, so how would you be sure you were carrying the right suitcase?

Oh, we would get into a lot of trouble if we all looked alike!

AS THINGS REALLY ARE

it is all much more convenient. Even if you have to meet an aunt whom you've never seen before, it is pretty easy to find her. There are all sorts of ways of describing people.

Are they light or dark? Are they tall or short, fat or thin? Do they have blue eyes or brown, black, gray, or green? Is their hair curly or straight, and what color is it? Are there moles on their chins or freckles on their cheeks? And noses—oh, my, think of all the different kinds of noses people can have: flat or sharp or narrow or hooked or pug.

Yes, it is a very lucky thing for all of us that we don't look alike.

And there is no place in the whole world where all people in that place look exactly alike.

THE COLOR OF SKIN

makes a difference in the way people look. It is probably the first thing we notice about someone's looks.

We sometimes say: "There goes a black man" or "He is a white man." We don't stop to think that we aren't really describing the color of the skin. For no one looks perfectly white—as white as paper. No one looks perfectly black—as black as shoes. You can't even describe skin by saying that it is brown or tan or pink or yellow. There are all kinds of different shades of color in the skin. Look down at your own hand and you will see that.

Doctors have been studying to find out what gives skin its color. They have found out, too. It is two chemicals.

"Melanin" (*mel*-a-nin) is the name of the chemical that gives the brown color to the skin.

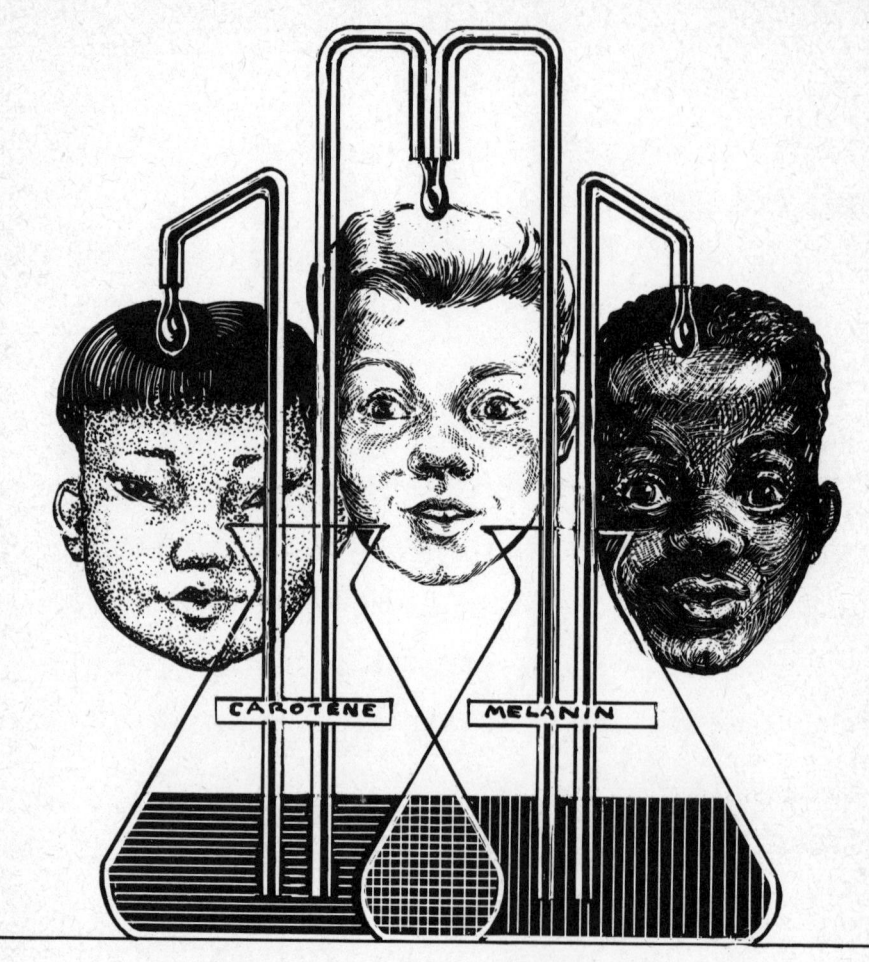

The color of a person is just skin-deep

"Carotene" (*car*-o-tene) is the chemical that gives the yellowish color.

Each one of us has some of both of these chemicals in our skin. Sometimes there is more melanin, sometimes more carotene. Except for the red blood vessels that shine through and give a pinkish tint to the skin your color is made by the mixing of these two chemicals.

This is the way it works: a person who happens to have a lot of melanin in his skin will be brown. A person with a lot of carotene in his skin will be yellow-tan. And someone with just a little melanin and just a little carotene, with skin thin enough for the blood vessels to show through, will be a pinkish, tannish white.

Very simple, isn't it? The names of the two chemicals may be hard to remember and harder still to spell, but the whole idea is easy. Just remember when you are looking at someone's skin color, that everyone has some of both the melanin and the carotene in their skins. It's just a matter of how much.

After a summer of being out in the sun—on a beach or in the cornfields or on a baseball lot—all of us have more melanin in our skins. That's what a sun-tan is. The freckles that sometimes dot our arms and make a little path across the bridge of our noses are just little spots of skin that have a lot of melanin in them.

Now that you have learned two such high-sounding words, you can show off. When you see a brown-skinned man walking down the street, you won't say: "There goes a black man." *You* can say (if you care to mention it at all): "There goes a man with a lot of melanin in his skin."

And if you should see a Chinese or an American Indian, you can say (although it is not very important): "There goes a man with a lot of carotene in his skin."

I suppose all you can say about a white man is that he is someone with not much melanin and not much carotene, but pale-skinned instead! American Indians used to call white men "palefaces"; and that is just what they are.

Of course, as you know very well, the color of a person is just skin deep. That isn't very deep either when you remember how easy it is to skin your knee. A brown boy who falls down on gravel, and a yellow boy who falls down on gravel, and a white boy who falls there too, all have the same kind of red-skinned places on their knees.

They all hurt just exactly the same, too.

HAIR IS DIFFERENT, TOO.

It can be red or yellow, gray, brown or black, besides all of the colors in-between. It can be very straight, or very curly, or just a little wavy instead.

And guess what? Your old friend melanin is right there in the hair, too. That same chemical gives color to the strands of hair.

When the hair has a lot of melanin in it, you have black or brown hair. The less melanin, the lighter the hair. Carotene is missing when it comes to hair-coloring, but you must meet a new one: the red color. It isn't present in the skin, but it is in some hair. Melanin and the red coloring in all different kinds of mixtures give the different shades of red and brown and blond hair. Of course, when there is no color at all, the hair is white.

Each tiny hair is a certain shape, too. You can't see the shape unless you look at it under a microscope strong enough to make the hair strands seem very large. But if you should cut strands of hair from a lot of different heads and put the ends under a microscope you could see these differences in shape. Some ends would look round, and you would find that they came from strands of hair that were straight. Some would look oval like an egg. They would come from strands that were curly. Some would look like a very flat circle, and they would come from hair that was extremely curly.

Most people have hair that is in-between — not perfectly straight, not terribly curly. Some of it is straighter than the rest; some of it is curlier, as you can see very well when you look into a mirror.

All About Us

And anyhow the really important thing is that hair, straight or curly, grows out of heads. You may have been thinking all along that all heads were the same shape—except for people with "the big head," of course.

Heads have to be measured

But some people have long heads, and some people have round heads, and some people have heads that are in-between. It is hard to tell just by looking at a person whether he is round-headed or long-headed. Heads have to be measured to find out. They are measured with a very special kind of ruler by people who have had to learn how.

They measure the head sideways, and then they measure it longways, and after that they do some arithmetic. The answer they get tells whether the person they have been measuring has a round head or a long head.

When they have finished it doesn't really mean a thing except that they know the shapes of some heads.

People used to think that the shape of the head was important. If Mr. Tigglebog had a round head and all of his relations and his wife and children had round heads, then he thought that everyone who had a long head wasn't as smart as he was. For Mr. Tigglebog (just like you and me!) wanted to feel that he was more important than anyone else.

If Mr. Sigglegog had a long head, then he thought that everyone who had a round head was dull or bad or worse. Because Mr. Sigglegog (and don't forget us!) wanted to be the best.

These ideas probably got about because the brain is inside the head. And it was thought that the size and shape of the brain had something to do with the way it worked. But now we know that some of the smartest men in the world have had the smallest brains; and the largest brain in the world ever found belonged to an idiot.

The shape of the person's head has nothing at all to do with the manners he has or the color of his skin or the way he walks and talks. It hasn't anything to do with how good his brains are or whether he is smart or "dumb."

It's lucky that they have found that out, too. Because it would be pretty silly to have to measure a boy's head before you could tell whether he was good enough to play on your baseball team. It would be just as silly as looking to see how much melanin or carotene he had in his skin before you could have him for a friend.

BLOOD CAN BE DIFFERENT,

but not in the way some people think. Every day you hear people say things like this:

"He has Indian blood in him."

"She comes of some of the finest blood in the country."

"He has bad blood — that is the reason he acts that way."

"We are blood relations."

"She has a little colored blood."

All this kind of talk sounds as if different people have blood of different colors. You know very well, of course, that you can prick a person's finger and look at the blood, but you will never in the world find out anything at all about him from that. The blood won't tell you whether his grandfather was rich, or whether he was born in a foreign country, or whether he goes to a Jewish church, or whether he has a brown skin.

Blood is the same no matter where you live, or where your grandmother lived, except that each person has blood of a certain type.

Doctors learned about these types when they began to give blood transfusions to help sick people.

There are four types of blood, and their names are: O, A, B, and AB. Type O can be mixed with any of the other types, but the rest can't be mixed with each other, or the sick person will die.

But anyone can have A or O or AB or B type of blood. These types can be found all over the world among all kinds of people if you care to look for them.

Even people in the same family do not have the same type of blood although we inherit our blood type from one of our grandparents. You might inherit your type of blood from your great-grandmother on your father's side, and your sister might inherit hers from your great-grandfather on your mother's side.

The color of the skin, the shape of the head, whether the hair is straight or curly, has nothing to do with the type of blood a person has.

They all can have the same blood type

THE FACT IS

people look different from one another. There are tall people and short people everywhere in the world. There are people with big feet, and people with flat feet, and people whose feet hurt all of the time. Blue-eyed and brown-eyed people, round and almond-eyed people live everywhere all over the world.

And anyone can tell just by looking that we don't all have the same kind of noses. They are all useful for smelling, but there is one thing to remember. The shape of the nose cannot tell us a thing about the kind of church the person goes to, or whether he would be fun to play with. Scottish people who go to the Presbyterian church often have exactly the same kind of nose as Polish people who go to the Jewish church or Italian people who go to the Catholic church.

It is the same way for all of the things that make us look different. They are only on the outside. They have nothing to do with the insides of us. If looking a certain way had anything to do with getting rich or being smart, we might all try to look the same. As it is, we don't have to worry about that.

It's a good thing, too.

It would be so silly if we all looked alike.

About
THE WAY WE ACT

CHAPTER III

The train goes backward and forward

WE DON'T ALL ACT ALIKE

just as we don't all look alike. But the way we look hasn't anything at all to do with the way we act. People used to think it did, though.

When the Biggles met the Sogs after being separated so long, they not only thought the Sogs looked funny; they thought they acted funny, too. They thought the food they ate was queer, and that the clothes they wore were queerer, and that the way they talked was the queerest of all. Because the Biggles couldn't understand a word the Sogs said!

The Biggles and the Siggles thought that the way they spoke and did things was the only way. The Sogs and Gogs thought that the way they spoke and acted was the only way. And there were the Biggle-Sogs and the Siggle-Gogs who thought everyone was pretty queer unless they talked like them and did things their way.

Everyone thought that the others talked and acted

queer because they *looked* different. They thought that brown people talked differently and ate differently because they had brown skin. They didn't know that a person who lives in a certain place copies the ways of the people around him. People change their ways of talking and acting, even though they can't change the color of their skins.

People who have the same kinds of manners and dress often speak different languages. And on the other hand, sometimes people who speak the same language have very different manners. An English boy says "lamb chop" just as you do, but he doesn't eat it the same way. You may have been taught to hold your fork in your left hand when you cut the meat, and to change it over to your right hand when you are ready to eat it. But the English and many people who live here hold their forks with their left hand while they are cutting, and they keep it right there for eating.

Our manners, our dress, our language started in the times of long ago. They began because of the way people lived in a particular place. Most of the things we do are copied from those people and those times.

LET'S PRETEND

that we are going on a trip. The train we will take is not an ordinary one. It is a very queer train indeed.

When you take a trip on a regular train to California, you go to the ticket office and buy a ticket to San Francisco. (That is, if you have the money.) When the time comes, you get on that train and ride and ride until you get to the place where you are going.

But our train is different. It goes backward and forward over land and sea. It goes backward and forward into time.

For instance, you can go to the ticket window of our funny train's station and say: "I want a ticket to see George Washington." And before you know it, you are on a train that is taking you from now back to 1797; from wherever you are to Washington's home at Mt. Vernon, Virginia.

That's quite a train, isn't it?

Well, what are we waiting for? Let's get on. We aren't visiting General Washington, though. We must travel hundreds of years backward in time. We must go thousands of miles across the ocean to England.

Watch out! We're stopping! Here we are. Now, look out of the window!

The castle stands high on the hillside. It is long and low and can barely be seen above the high stone wall that surrounds it. Below the wall and on the outside there is a ditch filled with water. The ditch is to keep enemies from coming through the wall gates.

As you watch, the big gates in the high wall are opened. A bridge is let down over the ditch, and a man rides out. His name is Sir Bigglety. He is on a big strong horse. And he needs a big strong horse, because Sir Bigglety is heavy and his suit and sword are heavier.

Sir Bigglety is wearing a suit of armor. It is not made of cloth; it is made of iron. It catches the sun like a mirror, and you almost have to shade your eyes to look at it. The suit is worn to keep Sir Bigglety's enemies from cutting him up with their swords.

Sir Bigglety rides bravely out over his fields. He is the only moving thing on the landscape, until suddenly, far off, another man appears, riding on a big strong horse. And this man needs a strong horse for the very same reason that Sir Bigglety needs one. He has on a suit of armor that reflects the sunlight, and he wears it to protect himself from his enemies.

What is going to happen? You see, Sir Bigglety has had a very big breakfast that morning of a whole leg of lamb and a good-sized piece of roast pork, and a lot of sweetened water to wash it down. He is not feeling at all like getting into a fight. All he wants to do is ride over the fields on his big strong horse while his brightly polished suit of clothes sparkles in the sun.

Sir Bigglety doesn't want to fight, but he doesn't

want to be cut up either. He is too far away to call out to the other knight that he is a friendly man. Any minute now he might dash at Sir Bigglety with his long sword ready to strike.

You may think you are going to see a fight, but you aren't. Sir Bigglety does what he has learned to do in such cases. He quickly puts his sword into his left hand and holds out his right hand to show that there is no weapon in it. And that is a sign that Sir Bigglety doesn't want to fight. It shows that he wants to be friends.

Whoosh! the train is moving again! This time it is speeding forward—forward hundreds of years into now, forward thousands of miles into here. Watch out! We're going to stop. Here we are! Look out of the window!

The drug store stands on the corner, and opposite it is the Middletown Grocery Store; down a little way is the Middletown Hardware Company. There are trees along the sidewalk and electric light poles spaced evenly between.

As you watch, the door of the drug store opens, and a lone man walks out. His name is Mr. Sigglety. He walks quickly and easily because his clothes are light and cool, and on his head he wears a straw hat. The straw hat is to keep the sun from burning his bald spot.

He is the only moving thing on the street, until suddenly from around the corner another lone man appears. This other man walks quickly, too, because his clothes are light and cool, and on his head he wears a straw hat. The straw hat is to cover *his* bald spot.

What is going to happen? Well, nothing at all. Mr. Sigglety has just finished a fine breakfast of orange juice and ham and eggs with some hot coffee for washing it down. But even if he had had no breakfast at all, he wouldn't feel like fighting. He is feeling very friendly indeed.

Mr. Sigglety puts out his right hand and shakes hands with his friend, just as he has been taught to do.

Shaking hands is a sign of friendship

It is doubtful if Mr. Sigglety knows that he shakes hands because Sir Bigglety of long, long ago, was afraid he might get cut up in a fight. But the reason Mr. Sigglety shakes hands is that everyone who lives where he lives does it. We happen to live in a part of the world where shaking hands is a sign of friendliness.

Tipping hats started in much the same way. Knights of old who went riding in heavy armor, just as Sir Bigglety did, often raised the little door that covered their faces to show their friends that there was a smile on their faces instead of a snarl.

Nowadays, when Mr. Tigglebog walks down the street tipping his hat to all the ladies he meets, he probably doesn't know that he is doing it because a knight was feeling in a friendly mood.

The way we show friendliness hasn't a thing to do with the color of our skins or whether our hair is curly or not. If we happened to be in a part of the world where rubbing noses was a sign of friendliness, we'd learn to rub noses.

For who wants to be without friends?

WE LEARN HOW TO ACT

by copying what other people around us do. That is the way we learn to use forks and knives and dishes. That is the reason we wear the kind of clothes we wear and live in the kinds of houses we live in and eat the sort of foods we have for our dinners. That is the way we learn words and sentences and how to talk. That is the way we learn the meanings of certain gestures and how to use them.

You may not believe it, but that is the way we also learn how to be polite and impolite, when to cry, and even the proper way of fighting and making up afterwards.

Men who are trying to be extra polite walk on the outside of the sidewalk next to the street when they are with ladies. Do you know why? It first started in the places where people just threw all their dirty water and waste stuff out of their upstairs front windows. It would land on the men instead of the ladies they were taking for a walk. And later men protected their ladies from the mud that might spatter up from the unpaved streets.

Now, of course, most streets are paved. You very rarely find anyone throwing his garbage out of the upstairs windows. But men still think that the outside of the sidewalk is the proper place to walk.

People threw all their dirty water and waste —

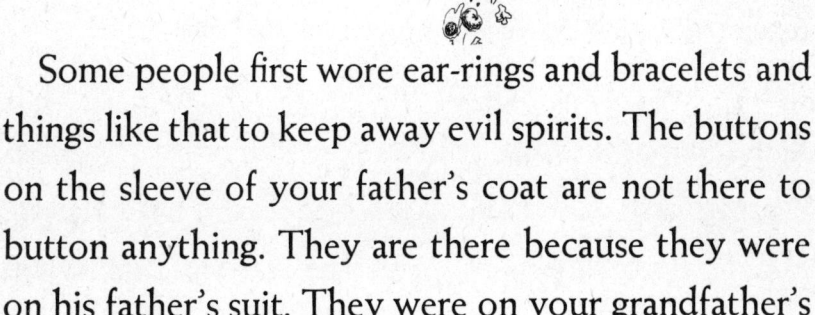

Some people first wore ear-rings and bracelets and things like that to keep away evil spirits. The buttons on the sleeve of your father's coat are not there to button anything. They are there because they were on his father's suit. They were on your grandfather's

— it would land on the men instead

suit because they were on *his* father's suit. You can go on back and back until you get to the first time when buttons on sleeves were used—to keep soldiers from wiping their noses on them! At least that's what the stories say.

When you were a baby and you threw your cup of milk on the floor, your mother would shake her head from side to side and say: "No! No!"

But when you kept it neatly on the tray of your high chair and didn't spill a drop, she would nod her head up and down and say: "Yes! Yes! That's right!"

Before you knew it, you had learned that when you mean "No," you must shake your head from side to side. When you mean "Yes," you must nod your head up and down.

But if you went on a visit to see Joe in Abyssinia, for instance, he wouldn't know what to think when you said "No" by shaking your head. For he says it by jerking his head over his right shoulder, and he says "Yes" by throwing his head straight back. Of course, Joe Abyssinia does that because his mother taught him to do it that way, just as Joe America does the other way because he learned it from *his* mother.

Or, if you are visiting Joe Borneo, he raises his eyebrows to say "Yes" and draws these eyebrows close together to say "No."

And it would be very confusing to talk to Joe New Zealand and Joe Sicily at the same time, because one raises his head and chin to say "Yes," and the other does the very same thing to say "No."

All of them do it their own way because they are copying their mothers and fathers and neighbors, who have copied their grandfathers and grandmothers and their neighbors.

When Joe Borneo or Joe Sicily come to see Joe America they very soon learn the way it is done over here. The shape of their heads or noses, the size of their feet or the color of their skin have nothing at all to do with the way they say "Yes" or "No."

Or take the matter of crying, for instance. When we are hurt or sorry or sad, it feels good to cry. It helps us to feel better. But an Indian child is very much ashamed to cry. He learns early that it is something to be ashamed of, and so he just doesn't cry. When an African child hurts himself, he feels a lot better if no one sees him. But most of us feel a lot better if someone does.

Fighting is another thing that is done differently in different parts of the world. When you get mad at Johnny Sigglegog, what do you do? Most likely you get a snarl on your face, you stick out your chin, you raise your fists and growl, and then you may hit him a fast one on the chin.

You fight that way because people where you live have always done that when they get mad.

But Jimmy Lopez, who happens to be an Indian of South America, fights in a very different way. When he gets mad at someone, he picks up a stick, and the other boy picks up a stick. They take their sticks to a rock and begin hitting the rock and not each other. It's all the same to the rock, and it doesn't hurt Jimmy Lopez and his friend a bit.

They whack at this rock with all their might, and

They hit the rock and not each other

all of the time they yell names at each other. They do this until one stick breaks, and then the fight is over. That's all there is to it. The one whose stick breaks first is the winner.

Of course, those Indian boys fight that way because the people where they live have always done that when they got mad.

The Eskimos have a good but different way of settling bigger fights, too. If two different villages get mad at each other, they don't arm themselves with weapons and have a war. They sing! That's really all they do. They just sing.

One village will make up insulting songs and the other village will make up insulting songs. Then they meet at a special place and sing them to each other. Judges are chosen to see which songs are the most insulting, and who wins the battle. Sometimes the judges can't decide for a long time, and so day after day the two villages sing to each other. A very long and musical war!

And they all sing

The Plains Indians, who look something like the Eskimos, liked to fight in wars. Their children learned to fight just as Eskimo children were taught to fish for seal and to make up insulting songs. Indian chiefs would make up little parties and go on the war path just so their young men could get a little practice in fighting a war.

Some cannibal tribes think war is very silly, because why should people want to kill other people unless they are hungry?

And there are other tribes who fight in wars, but stop fighting as soon as one warrior is killed. The side that kills him wins the battle.

There are still others who think war is such fun that they will even give their enemies food and weapons so that they can keep on fighting.

But the Eskimos think the whole idea of having a war is stupid. Who knows, maybe some day all of us will be thinking the same thing.

We get most of our ideas and ways of acting from our grandmothers and grandfathers who have gone before us. But we keep learning new ways, too. We learn new ways because of new inventions. Our great grandmothers wore wide hoop skirts, but what would happen to a crowded bus or street car or train if all the ladies' skirts took up most of the room?

We learn from the different people who come to live with us. We learn from visiting people in their different home lands.

For since people began, they have traveled; and as they traveled, they have learned.

About
AMERICANS

CHAPTER IV

They came from all kinds of places—

DOWN THROUGH THE AGES,
the peoples of the earth have wandered over the globe. They may have settled down for several hundreds of years in one place, but after a while some Mr. Alfred Biggle would decide to go traveling. And with him would go his wife and children and some of their friends and relations.

Sometimes these brave and adventurous people went to places that had never seen a human face—to earth that had never felt a human footstep.

America was a place like that. For we don't know how many thousands of years there was no person here at all. Elephants and over-sized buffaloes with long shaggy hair and huge tusks, deer with sharp-pointed horns and softly stepping feet had the freedom of our land. They thundered over the mountains and grazed quietly in our green valleys, without ever bumping into a human soul.

That was before the Biggle-Sogs found it, or whatever their names were. All we know is that the name certainly wasn't Columbus.

Yellowish-tan men, their skins burned red-brown by the sun, their straight black hair streaming in the wind, first stepped into the wilderness of America. They brought their families, too,—their light-brown wives, their black-haired children, with slant eyes opened wide to the new sights. They brought their dogs!

No one knows exactly how they came. Most of them came from the northeastern part of Asia we call Siberia. Maybe there was a bridge of land from Siberia to Alaska. If there was, then these people could have come on foot. And if there was no land bridge, then they could have crossed from Siberia to Alaska on the ice. The Bering Straits (which is the water that separates these two lands now) are only a few miles across, and even now the water in these Straits sometimes freezes hard enough during the winter so that people could walk all the way from Siberia to Alaska, if they were strong enough. So these early Americans may have come on the ice.

No one knows why they came either. But we can be rather sure that they went traveling for the same reason that most people wandered the earth, because they were hungry. They were probably looking for something to eat. They were almost certainly not looking for a beautiful country where you and I could live and go to school and work and have fun. The Biggle-Sogs were almost certainly not thinking about us at all.

We don't know how long it took them to come. It is sure to have taken a long time. Some of them stopped up in the cold country of Alaska and became the people we know as Eskimos. Some of them came down to what is now the United States. Others wandered further south to the high and lofty mountains, the soft and sunny skies of Mexico. They became the people whom Columbus called the Indians.

They were the first Americans. Most of us, as well as our great-great-grandmothers and grandfathers, came here much later.

We came uninvited to the Indians' land.

But because the Indians were here and had been here for thousands of years, it was a better America. In the first place, the Indians knew a lot about living here that the newcomers didn't know. They had learned to grow some special foods; they had learned which animals and birds were good to eat, and how to track them down. These reddish-tan men (with carotene in their skin, remember?) who first stepped into America had to teach those of us who came much later how to live here.

They didn't teach us to fight them, though. We did that all by ourselves. The Indians wanted to keep their own villages and farms and houses that they had worked so hard to build. We wanted their land. We had guns so we pushed the Indians out of their homes.

Sometimes today, we feel that the Indians don't even belong in America. We sometimes forget that it was their country first.

PEOPLE KEPT ON TRAVELING,

and many people from many lands came to the United States. If they hadn't come, where would you and I be? We certainly wouldn't be *here!*

People came here because they were hungry and because there was no way to get enough food in their own lands. They came because they did not like their kings and wanted more freedom. They came because they were tired of the old ways of doing things and wanted to try a new life in a new land.

Most of the people who came to America came because they wanted to come. They decided quite by themselves that they wanted to live in the New World. So they built their own boats. Or they saved money and bought passage on the sailing ships that were willing to risk the dangers of the ocean voyage.

But there were some people who came because they were made to come. In England there were people so poor that they gave themselves as slaves to richer men in order to get food and a place to live. These bondservants had to do what their masters told them to do.

They were sold to other men

They were even sold to other men who could do with them as they wanted. Many of them were forced to come here to work in the fields of Virginia and North Carolina.

These English people were the grandmothers and grandfathers of many people who live in America today.

As the first settlers began to grow more and more tobacco and cotton, they needed more and more people to work in the fields. As they began to build more and more houses and barns and towns, they needed more and more workers. The supply of bond-servants began to give out.

That is why ships sailed along the coast of Africa. That is why men from those ships went into the little green villages of Africa, into the happy green farm lands, and kidnapped men and women and children to work in the new land.

and kidnapped men, women and children

The people whom they captured and took from their own homes were farmers and carpenters and musicians. They were merchants and wood-carvers and weavers. Some of them had been kings in their own lands. Some had been the wise men of their tribes: the teachers, the poets, and the doctors.

When they got here they were sold into slavery. And they were the grandfathers and grandmothers of many of the Negroes who live in America today.

AMERICA KEPT GROWING.

Men began to build better and safer ships. Men began to clear the forests and plant the land farther and farther to the west. From the Atlantic Ocean to the Pacific Ocean people were pushing into new places.

The people who did this, who rode in the covered wagons, who opened the water-ways, who built the railroads and great cities all over our country, were people who came here in ships from other lands.

They came from all kinds of places with all kinds of

faces and all kinds of ways of doing and saying things. They came from Spain and England and France. They came from Russia and Germany and Sweden. They came from Scotland and Ireland, from Italy and Turkey. There was no place from which they did not come — from the rice fields and crowded cities of China, from the rocky coasts and deep and narrow inlets of Norway.

They were all different — these people from so many different lands. At least they were different before they came to the New World. After they got here, they were all alike in one way. They were alike bcause they were all Americans.

Being an American has nothing at all to do with the place a person lived before. Being American has nothing at all to do with the way a person looks. Americans are the people—all of the people—who came here to live.

It would not be the same America if the Spanish and English and the French had not come. There would not be the America we love if the Dutch or the

Russians or the Africans had not come. And it would certainly not be the place it is now if the Indians had not been here already.

It doesn't make much difference either, whether Americans came in 1600 or whether they came in 1942. The only important thing is that they did come and that we are all here now.

About
OUR FRIENDS

CHAPTER V

WOULDN'T IT BE SILLY

if we liked everybody in exactly the same way? That would be as silly as wanting everyone to look exactly alike. That would be as dull as wanting everyone to act exactly alike.

You wouldn't have any special boy or girl friends. You wouldn't have any favorite cousins or aunts or uncles. You would like a certain Mr. and Mrs. Super-Sniggle as much as you like your own father and mother.

It would really be a queer state of affairs. But it isn't like that at all. And no one wants it to be. We choose our own friends. We decide which people we want to love. The people that you choose to like might not be at all the kind that I choose to like.

It is very lucky that we don't all like exactly the same kind of people. But have you ever stopped to think about how you select your friends?

Do you choose your friends because of the way they look? You may not, but many do. They sometimes choose a special someone for a friend only because he looks a certain way.

There may be some of us who wouldn't make friends with a boy who has a lot of melanin in his skin. There are sure to be some of us who wouldn't be friends with people whose skin has a lot of carotene in it. And, of course, there are some who won't get acquainted with people who have only a little melanin and carotene in their outside covering.

Choosing your friends is really up to you. We don't all like the same kinds of people. But sometimes we miss a lot when we don't find out what people are like on the *inside*, because we are too busy looking at the *outside*.

You may live in a neighborhood where all of the people are white. Johnnie Johnson moves in, and Johnnie Johnson happens to be a Negro. That is, his skin is brown and his hair is black and his nose is flatter than it is sharp.

Maybe at the same time Jack Smith moves on your street too, and Jack Smith happens to be white like you. That is, his skin is sort of whitish and his hair is light brown and his nose is little and turned up at the end.

Here are two new boys your own age in your neighborhood. They might make good additions to the gang that is building a clubhouse on the vacant lot at the end of the street. They might be good members for a ball team that needs to win some games. But what do you do?

You look over Jack Smith as a possible member of your team and your gang. You say "Hello" to him and you ask him where he's from and what grade he's in and things like that. Maybe you like him; maybe you don't. If not, then he isn't invited to join you on Saturday mornings. But at least you have found out whether you might like him or not.

There is Johnnie Johnson. You stare at him, but you don't speak. You don't find out anything at all about him. You don't know whether he is a good catcher or whether he has an old radio of his own that he can fix for the clubhouse. If you had treated Johnnie as you have treated Jack, you might have discovered that you liked him or that you didn't like him. But you have never given yourself the chance to find out.

Now, you and you may happen to live on a street where all of the people are Negroes. Charlie Lowe moves down the block from you, and Charlie Lowe happens to be Chinese. That is, his skin is yellow-tan and his hair is black and straight and his eyes are shaped like almonds.

Maybe at the same time, Henry Hendrickson moves on your street too, and Henry Hendrickson happens to be a Negro like you. That is, his skin is brown and his hair is curly and his eyes are black.

Here are two boys, and they might be fun to play with. But you find out pretty soon whether you want to walk to school with Henry and maybe get a soda afterwards when you have the money.

But you only stare at Charlie and you never find

out whether he plays a good game of marbles or can do tricks on his bicycle.

IF YOU CHOOSE YOUR FRIENDS

for the clothes they wear, the houses they live in, the country where they were born, or the church they attend, you may be missing a lot of fun. Until you get a chance to know people, you can't tell how you will feel about them.

Perhaps there were some people who felt rather ashamed after Abraham Lincoln became President. They could have been the people who hadn't wanted him for a friend because he lived in a log cabin and wore patched overalls.

How would you like to have a chance to talk to Joe Louis? His skin is brown and his clothes were poor when he was a little boy trying to go to school.

Who wouldn't brag about being friends with Edward G. Robinson or Charles Boyer or Hedy Lamarr? Well, they were all born in a foreign country.

Wouldn't you be proud to have Eddie Cantor's autograph? His parents most certainly went to a Jewish church.

You are lucky and probably have a better time than some of us if you choose your friends because they are easy to talk to, or like the same movies and victrola records, or have good ideas for games—or because they like you. You are very lucky if you don't have to think about anything else.

There are all sorts of good reasons for choosing friends. But the way people look or the amount of money they have or the country they came from or the church they go to are pretty silly reasons for not getting acquainted.

You may sometimes hear people say that they don't like Negroes or that they don't like Jews, or Catholics or foreigners.

Have you ever thought what a curious thing that is to say? How can anyone tell that he doesn't like Negroes? To say that he would have to know every single Negro in the United States. For we all know that we can't like or dislike someone until we know him.

How can anyone decide that he doesn't like Jews? That would be very hard, because you often can't tell them from anyone else. It is very hard to look at a person and tell at once that he goes to a certain church.

For a Jew is a person who goes to the Jewish church. Of course, many people are called Jews who never go to church. But they are spoken of that way because their parents or their grandparents followed the Jewish religion. There are people who go to this church living in every part of the world and with all kinds of different skin colors and nose shapes.

The people in this country whom you may think "look like Jews" are people from a certain part of Europe who may or may not go to the Jewish church. You would find it hard to tell an Italian who goes to the Catholic church from an Italian who goes to the Jewish church. One would be an Italian Catholic and one would be an Italian Jew. And I am sure that an

Italian Methodist could look almost exactly like either one of them.

As for hating foreigners, then we might as well hate ourselves! For all Americans, except the Indians are from a foreign land.

You might as well hate yourself!

SNOOTY PEOPLE

sometimes live next door to us. Sometimes they are in school with us or go to parties where we are trying to have fun or wait on us in grocery stores.

Snooty people are all the people who think they are better than other people. And they think they have very good reasons for always walking with their noses in the air.

Some people are snooty because they think they have more ancestors than anyone else. You know, even if some snooty Mrs. Super-Sniggle doesn't, that we all had the same great-great-great grandfathers and grandmothers. Mrs. Super-Sniggle couldn't possibly have more than you or I because we all had the same number.

All of us had the same first grandfathers and grandmothers. We were descended from them as well as the children in Borneo and West Africa and Russia and Japan. So while Mrs. Super-Sniggle is counting her ancestors we could be counting ours, too. We would all get the same answer, although you and I are much too busy to spend our time bothering about *that*.

And then there are snooty people who think they are better than other people because their ancestors were white. They think that white grandfathers are the grandest of all. That snooty Mrs. Van Tiggleworth must have had some very wonderful ancestors. But it is stupid of her to think that hers were better than brown or yellow-tan ancestors. For at the time that the Van Tiggleworth white grandfather of long ago was wearing a piece of animal fur around him for a suit, brown people living in parts of Africa were weaving fine cloth. Grandfather Van Tiggleworth was eating berries and roots while the people who lived along the banks of the Nile in Egypt had learned that there was no sense in wandering over the earth looking for food when they could stay in one place and grow it. They were making iron tools and plows to till the land. They were making bricks and houses from those bricks all of the time the Van Tiggleworth ancestors were living in caves.

Of course, none of this was the fault of anybody. It doesn't mean that the Africans were smarter than the Van Tiggleworths, or that the Van Tiggleworths couldn't have been as smart as the Egyptians. People learned different things at different times.

All of us know people who are snooty because they have white skins. But they seem to forget why they are white.

Of course they have white skins because their fathers and mothers have white skins. The snooty people had nothing at all to do with it; they had no way of choosing their fathers and mothers; they just happened to be born that way.

They had no way of choosing their parents

We all know that the two chemicals—carotene and melanin decide the color of the skin. We also know that a skin that doesn't have much of either one of those chemicals in it is, after all, just a skin even if it is white. It covers our flesh and bones and that is all it is good for. It has nothing to do with our insides or our brains. It has something to do with our looks, but so has red hair or big feet or a pug nose.

Can you imagine people being snooty because they have big feet?

You may know a snooty Susie who is stuck up because her ancestors landed in this country a long time ago. She may think she is more American than anyone else because her great-great-great-grandfathers came over here when there were very few people in this land.

She doesn't like to sit next to Maria Lopez because Maria is from Mexico and is a "foreigner." The history books should tell this snooty Susie that Maria's great-great-great-grandfathers had built beautiful cities on our continent long before Susie's grandfathers ever thought of coming here. Susie doesn't seem to know it, but Maria is really more American than she is.

Susie sometimes makes fun of people who haven't a nice American name like Super-Sniggle or Van Tiggleworth. She might giggle at Ivan Ivanoff because he does not speak his English words in just the way Susie speaks. She is almost always snooty to Domi-

All About Us

You may know a Snooty Susie —

nico Romano because his lunch box is filled with different sorts of food from the kind in Susie's box.

Susie is snooty to Ivan and Dominico because they are "foreign."

Poor Susie hasn't stopped to think. For Susie's teacher can tell her that if we should be snooty to people who came to this country later than her grandfathers came—then the Indians ought to be snooty to Susie. If Ivan and Dominico are foreigners, it looks very much as if Susie is a foreigner, too, as

The Indians ought to be snooty to Susie

far as the Indians are concerned. Their grandfathers have been here longer than hers.

Of course, not all of the snooty people in America are named Super-Sniggle or Van Tiggleworth. Sometimes they are called Evans and sometimes Cohen. Sometimes the name is Brown or Ivansky or Schuyler. Sometimes they have brown skins, sometimes yellow-tan, sometimes white. But whoever they are, let's hope they soon get their heads down out of the air and their noses in their proper places.

Otherwise they will have to go stumbling through the world missing a lot of good times and good friends and not seeing what there is to see.

AMERICA IS A WONDERFUL PLACE

because of the people who live here. It is wonderful because of the people who have come and because of the people who keep coming from the lands across the sea. For all of the people who have come here to live have brought something with them.

Sometimes they brought new foods or new ways of cooking foods. Sometimes they brought new machines or tools to make new machines. They have brought the skill to paint beautiful pictures or make breath-taking music from a piano or violin. They have brought new ways of curing the sick. They have brought wonderful new inventions and beautiful words to go into books.

If you ever feel like saying that you hate any of the kinds of people who have come to America, then you must remember that you are saying that you hate America itself. For it would be very queer to like our buildings or our trains, our radios or our books, our movies or our games, the food we eat, the way we dress, while we hate any of the Americans who gave them to us.

All sorts and kinds of people came to America where the Indians were living by themselves. All sorts and colors and shapes and sizes of people came. All kinds of languages and manners and foods came with them.

All of us are Americans. All of us make the America we call our home.

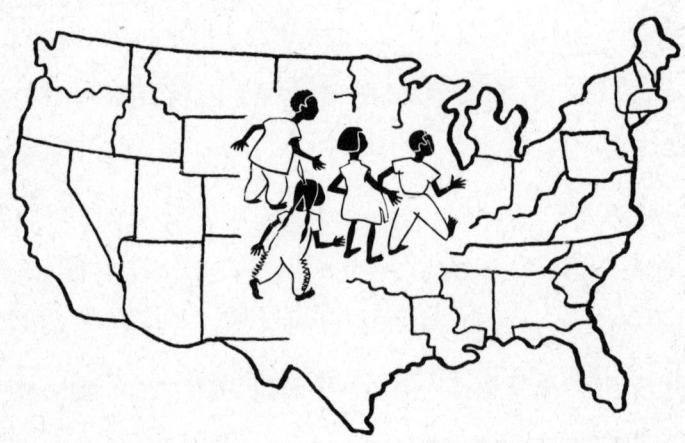

PEOPLE ARE IMPORTANT.

They are the most important thing in the whole world. They are much more important than fine houses and good clothes and spending money. They are worth a lot more than bicycles or catchers' mitts or ice cream sodas. People are more valuable than ponies and dogs and cats, than boats and automobiles, than fried chicken dinners and trips on trains.

People are so special, because they are US!

People began with the first men and women over a million years ago. They were the great-
              great-
                            no-one-knows-how-many-greats-grandmothers and grandfathers of all the peoples in the world today.

These first men and women were our great-grandmothers and grandfathers. They were the grandmothers and grandfathers of the people who live in China and Italy, and of all the people who live in

Brazil and Iceland, and in America and Turkey. We all had the same first grandfathers and grandmothers.

Every living person is kin to us, and we are related to everybody in the whole world.

Now you know
ALL ABOUT US

People are important